HOW TO ENHANCE YOUR SPIRITUAL LIFE

How to Enhance Your Spiritual Life

Walter the Educator

SKB
Silent King Books
A WhichHead Entertainment Imprint

Copyright © 2024 by Walter the Educator

All rights reserved. No part of this book may be reproduced in any manner whatsoever without written permission except in the case of brief quotations embodied in critical articles and reviews.

First Printing, 2024

Disclaimer

The author and publisher offer this information without warranties expressed or implied. No matter the grounds, neither the author nor the publisher will be accountable for any losses, injuries, or other damages caused by the reader's use of this book. Your use of this book acknowledges an understanding and acceptance of this disclaimer.

How to Enhance Your Spiritual Life is a little problem solver book by Walter the Educator that belongs to the Little Problem Solver Books Series.
Collect them all and more books at WaltertheEducator.com

LITTLE PROBLEM SOLVER BOOKS

INTRO

Spirituality is a deeply personal journey that often transcends religious practices or rituals. It represents the search for meaning, purpose, and connection to something greater than oneself, whether that be God, the universe, or the collective human experience. As we navigate the complexities of modern life, cultivating a vibrant spiritual life can bring inner peace, fulfillment, and clarity. Yet, enhancing your spiritual life requires intentionality, self-reflection, and openness to growth. This little book provides a comprehensive guide on how to enhance your spiritual life, offering practical steps, mindsets, and practices that can help deepen your connection to your spirituality.

How to Enhance Your Spirtual Life

1. Understand the Meaning of Spirituality

Before embarking on the journey of enhancing your spiritual life, it's important to first understand what spirituality means to you. Spirituality can take on various forms and interpretations based on individual experiences, beliefs, and cultural backgrounds. For some, spirituality is closely tied to religious practices, while for others, it may involve a connection to nature, personal growth, or inner peace.

How to Enhance Your Spirtual Life

Spirituality vs. Religion

While the terms "spirituality" and "religion" are often used interchangeably, they are not the same. Religion is typically structured around specific beliefs, doctrines, and rituals associated with a particular faith tradition. Spirituality, on the other hand, is more fluid and personal, focusing on the individual's inner experience and connection to the sacred or transcendent. You can be religious and spiritual, or you can pursue spirituality outside of formal religious frameworks.

How to Enhance Your Spirtual Life

Defining Your Spiritual Path

To enhance your spiritual life, it's helpful to reflect on what spirituality means to you. What do you feel connected to? What brings you a sense of peace, purpose, or meaning? Whether it's prayer, meditation, acts of service, or spending time in nature, understanding your spiritual path allows you to tailor your practices to align with your unique beliefs and values.

How to Enhance Your Spirtual Life

2. Cultivate Self-Awareness and Inner Reflection

At the heart of any spiritual journey is self-awareness. Enhancing your spiritual life requires a deep understanding of yourself, your thoughts, emotions, values, and desires. Self-awareness allows you to connect with your inner self, align your actions with your values, and recognize areas of your life that may need spiritual attention or growth.

How to Enhance Your Spirtual Life

Engage in Regular Self-Reflection

Self-reflection is a powerful tool for cultivating spiritual growth. By setting aside time to reflect on your thoughts, actions, and experiences, you can gain insight into your inner world and become more aware of patterns that may be affecting your spiritual life. Journaling is an effective way to practice self-reflection.

How to Enhance Your Spirtual Life

Writing down your thoughts, emotions, and experiences can help you process them and identify areas where you seek deeper meaning or connection.

How to Enhance Your Spirtual Life

Ask Yourself Deep Questions

To enhance your spiritual life, regularly ask yourself deep, introspective questions. What is my purpose? What are my core values? How do I want to contribute to the world? What brings me inner peace? By exploring these questions, you can gain clarity on your spiritual goals and take intentional steps toward spiritual growth.

How to Enhance Your Spirtual Life

Be Open to Change

Spiritual growth often requires change, whether it's changing your beliefs, habits, or the way you relate to others. Be open to evolving and adapting as you learn more about yourself and your spiritual path. Embracing change allows for a deeper, more authentic connection to your spirituality.

How to Enhance Your Spirtual Life

3. Practice Mindfulness and Presence

Mindfulness, the practice of being fully present in the moment, is a cornerstone of spiritual growth. When you're mindful, you can experience life more deeply, appreciate its beauty, and connect with the sacred in the present moment. Mindfulness allows you to step away from the distractions and anxieties of daily life and find peace in simply being.

How to Enhance Your Spirtual Life

Engage in Mindful Practices

Mindfulness can be cultivated through various practices, such as meditation, yoga, or mindful breathing. Meditation, in particular, helps calm the mind, reduce stress, and increase self-awareness, making it a powerful tool for spiritual growth.

How to Enhance Your Spirtual Life

Whether you meditate for a few minutes each day or engage in longer sessions, meditation allows you to connect with your inner self and create space for spiritual insights.

How to Enhance Your Spirtual Life

Yoga, which combines physical movement with mindfulness and breath control, is another practice that can deepen your spiritual connection. It helps you become more attuned to your body, mind, and spirit, fostering a sense of unity and balance.

How to Enhance Your Spirtual Life

Be Present in Daily Activities

Mindfulness doesn't have to be limited to formal practices. You can incorporate mindfulness into your daily activities by paying attention to the present moment.

How to Enhance Your Spirtual Life

Whether you're eating, walking, or spending time with loved ones, bring your full awareness to the experience. This simple shift in attention can transform mundane activities into opportunities for spiritual connection and growth.

How to Enhance Your Spirtual Life

Disconnect from Technology

In today's fast-paced digital world, it's easy to become consumed by technology and miss out on the present moment. Taking regular breaks from screens and social media can help you reconnect with your inner self and the world around you. Digital detoxes give you the space to reflect, rest, and be fully present in your spiritual practice.

How to Enhance Your Spirtual Life

4. Connect with Nature

Nature has long been a source of spiritual inspiration and healing. Many people feel a deep sense of connection to the divine or the sacred when they spend time in nature.

How to Enhance Your Spirtual Life

Whether it's walking in the woods, sitting by the ocean, or simply enjoying a quiet moment in your garden, nature offers a space for reflection, renewal, and spiritual connection.

How to Enhance Your Spirtual Life

Spend Time Outdoors

Make it a habit to spend time in nature regularly, whether it's through hiking, gardening, or simply taking a walk in the park.

How to Enhance Your Spirtual Life

Nature has a way of calming the mind and bringing you into the present moment, making it easier to connect with your spirituality. Notice the beauty around you, the trees, the sky, the sound of birds, and allow yourself to feel a sense of awe and gratitude for the natural world.

How to Enhance Your Spirtual Life

Practice Ecospirituality

Ecospirituality is the recognition of the spiritual connection between humans and the earth. It involves seeing nature not just as a resource but as a sacred entity that we are deeply connected to.

How to Enhance Your Spirtual Life

Practicing ecospirituality can enhance your spiritual life by fostering a sense of responsibility for the environment and a deeper appreciation for the interconnectedness of all living things.

How to Enhance Your Spirtual Life

You might engage in rituals or practices that honor the earth, such as planting a tree, participating in environmental conservation efforts, or offering prayers of gratitude for the natural world. Ecospirituality encourages you to live in harmony with nature, which can lead to a more fulfilling and spiritually aligned life.

How to Enhance Your Spirtual Life

5. Develop Compassion and Kindness

Compassion and kindness are central to many spiritual traditions and practices. When you cultivate a heart of compassion, you align yourself with the values of love, empathy, and connection to others. Developing compassion for yourself and others can deepen your spiritual life by fostering a sense of unity and oneness with humanity.

How to Enhance Your Spirtual Life

Practice Self-Compassion

Spiritual growth often involves confronting our imperfections and mistakes. It's important to approach yourself with kindness and understanding rather than self-judgment or criticism.

How to Enhance Your Spirtual Life

Self-compassion involves treating yourself with the same care and empathy that you would offer to a friend in times of difficulty. By practicing self-compassion, you create a safe and nurturing environment for spiritual growth, allowing you to face challenges with grace and resilience.

How to Enhance Your Spiritual Life

Show Kindness to Others

Kindness is a powerful spiritual practice that can bring you closer to the divine and to others. Acts of kindness, whether big or small, help create a positive ripple effect in the world.

How to Enhance Your Spirtual Life

By showing kindness to others, whether it's through volunteering, offering a helping hand, or simply being present for a friend, you strengthen your connection to the human experience and cultivate a sense of unity and love.

How to Enhance Your Spirtual Life

Engage in Loving-Kindness Meditation

Loving-kindness meditation is a spiritual practice that involves sending thoughts of love, compassion, and well-being to yourself and others. During the meditation, you repeat phrases such as "May I be happy," "May I be healthy," "May I be at peace," and extend these wishes to loved ones, acquaintances, and even those with whom you may have conflict. This practice helps develop compassion and empathy, deepening your spiritual connection to all living beings.

How to Enhance Your Spirtual Life

6. Engage in Spiritual Study and Learning

Another way to enhance your spiritual life is by seeking knowledge and understanding through spiritual study. Whether you study sacred texts, read spiritual books, or explore the teachings of different traditions, spiritual learning can provide valuable insights and guidance on your journey.

How to Enhance Your Spirtual Life

Explore Sacred Texts and Teachings

If you follow a particular religious or spiritual tradition, studying its sacred texts can deepen your understanding and connection to your faith. For example, Christians might read the Bible, Buddhists might study the teachings of the Buddha, and Hindus might explore the Bhagavad Gita. These texts often offer wisdom, moral guidance, and inspiration for spiritual growth.

How to Enhance Your Spiritual Life

Even if you don't adhere to a specific religion, exploring spiritual teachings from different traditions can provide valuable insights. You might study the works of spiritual teachers, philosophers, or mystics whose ideas resonate with you. Broadening your spiritual knowledge allows you to deepen your understanding of the divine and explore new perspectives on spirituality.

How to Enhance Your Spirtual Life

Attend Spiritual Workshops or Retreats

Attending spiritual workshops, classes, or retreats can provide opportunities for growth, community, and learning. Workshops and retreats often focus on specific spiritual practices, such as meditation, yoga, or prayer, and allow you to immerse yourself in an environment dedicated to spiritual exploration. Surrounding yourself with like-minded individuals and experienced teachers can inspire and support your spiritual journey.

How to Enhance Your Spirtual Life

Learn from Spiritual Mentors

Having a spiritual mentor or guide can be incredibly valuable on your spiritual journey. A mentor can offer wisdom, encouragement, and guidance as you navigate challenges and explore new spiritual practices. Whether it's a religious leader, a spiritual teacher, or a trusted friend, having someone who can support your growth can enhance your spiritual life.

How to Enhance Your Spirtual Life

7. Embrace Silence and Solitude

In our fast-paced world, silence and solitude are often undervalued. However, these moments of quiet can be deeply nourishing for your spiritual life. Silence allows you to tune out external distractions and tune into your inner self, creating space for reflection, prayer, or meditation.

How to Enhance Your Spirtual Life

Create a Sacred Space for Silence

To enhance your spiritual life, create a sacred space where you can retreat for moments of silence and solitude. This space might be a corner of your home, a quiet spot in your garden, or a place in nature where you feel at peace. Use this space to practice meditation, prayer, or simply to sit in silence. In these quiet moments, you can connect more deeply with your spirituality and find clarity, peace, and inspiration.

How to Enhance Your Spirtual Life

Practice Regular Silence

Incorporating regular moments of silence into your day can help deepen your spiritual connection. You might start your morning with a few minutes of quiet reflection, take a break during your day for silent meditation, or end your evening with a moment of silence before bed. These small practices of silence can create a sense of stillness and inner peace that enhances your overall spiritual well-being.

How to Enhance Your Spirtual Life

OUTRO

Enhancing your spiritual life is a deeply personal and transformative journey. It involves cultivating self-awareness, mindfulness, compassion, and a connection to something greater than yourself. Whether you find spiritual fulfillment through prayer, meditation, nature, or acts of kindness, the key is to approach your spiritual life with openness, intentionality, and a commitment to growth. By embracing practices such as self-reflection, mindfulness, connection with nature, and compassion for others, you can deepen your spiritual connection and find greater meaning, peace, and fulfillment in your life. Ultimately, enhancing your spiritual life is not about reaching a final destination but about embracing the ongoing journey of inner exploration and growth.

ABOUT THE CREATOR

Walter the Educator is one of the pseudonyms for Walter Anderson. Formally educated in Chemistry, Business, and Education, he is an educator, an author, a diverse entrepreneur, and he is the son of a disabled war veteran. "Walter the Educator" shares his time between educating and creating. He holds interests and owns several creative projects that entertain, enlighten, enhance, and educate, hoping to inspire and motivate you. Follow, find new works, and stay up to date with Walter the Educator™

at WaltertheEducator.com

Milton Keynes UK
Ingram Content Group UK Ltd.
UKHW021938281024
450365UK00018B/1153